Reflections

Anne Seebaldt

© Anne Seebaldt 2014

ISBN 978-0-578-13530-4

This book of poetry is dedicated to the following people: Gram, Ruth Magdalen LaBerge, Grandpa, Edward Seebaldt, my parents, Barb and Ernie Seebaldt, my illustrator and first proofreader, Sarah Waldock, who kindly but firmly chivvied me through the process, to Michelle Chandler, who took on the unenviable task of editing an editor, to my final proofreaders, Mom (a.k.a. Barb), my cousin, Alan Clements, Jennifer Halls Saries and Candace Brancik, as well as to my goddaughter, Clare Palo (who plans to be a journalist, too) and to all the men I've loved and crushed on before (without whom half of these poems would not have been written).

Author's note: This little book is representative of my poetry over the last 30 years, arranged thematically.

I hope you enjoy reading them as much as I have enjoyed writing and revising them.

Contents

LOVE AND OTHER EMOTIONS

It's midnight and I am using a flashlight to light my pencil on the notebook because no one knows I'm up. I have to get that lyric down before it's out of my head. That was the way my poetry started, around about 1982-83, with the exception of school assignments. The poems always came when I was trying to sleep. Sometimes it felt like someone beyond my life experience was writing through me, which was rather creepy. I realized it was just inspiration, not possession, and learned to enjoy the times it decided to make an appearance. Strangely, when I went to revise *The Tides of Time* 30 years later, it didn't need as much work as I thought, which makes me feel a bit like my 16-year-old self had a crystal ball. Also creepy. Never mind. There's no way I had one of those. My klutzy teenage self would have broken it.

1983

The Tides of Time

Memories can wash you away
through the tides of time
To reflect on the peace and beauty
of "auld lang syne."

But time waits for no one.
Linger too long in the past,
and it will pass you by
like tides of the ocean,
like waves reflecting the sky.

Love can break through the tides of time
and float on throughout the years.
It lasts through good times and bad,
through laughter and tears.

Love can make the tides of time stand still;
it cuts right through the tides of time and always will.

So don't dwell too long in the past,
or maybe love will pass you by.
Take a chance, now; go for it!
Don't sit there and just sigh
all through the tides of time.

1984

Below is my first-ever published poem; in 1984, it was printed in *The Milford Times'* Poets Corner.

I Wish

I wish I was a bee,
or a butterfly or nymph.
Instead, I am merely human.
I wish I could be special.

I wish I had some incredible talent.
I wish I could be someone
quite different from the ordinary self
I see reflected in the mirror.

Danny was an off-duty Oakland County Sheriff's deputy, one of my cousin's best friends and a family friend who was killed in a car accident up north during my junior year of high school, primarily because he was not wearing his seatbelt. It is why I am so insistent everyone in my car wears one. His death hit me quite hard; I had a massive crush on him.

Why Danny?

He was taken away.
Why couldn't he stay?
Why Danny?

He was such a good friend.
Why did his life end?
Why Danny?

He was so good and so kind.
The world's lost him —
I think I'm losing my mind.
Tell me: why Danny?

God, please tell me why
Did Danny have to die?
I can't understand — why Danny?

Everyone loved him.
He loved them too.
Why Danny? I wonder.
Why you?

Why do we love?
Loving always gives us pain.
Are we just mortal fools?
Danny won't come this way again.

He died so young …
He'd just turned 24.
Only the good die young, you see.

But I still don't understand … why Danny?

Parting is sheer sorrow, far from sweet
But life must go on.
There are new challenges to meet
But they'll be without Danny.

Why is the sun shining?
How can the birds be singing
when the world has lost Danny?
Why take him from us?

It seems I shouldn't laugh; I can't sing.
I can only cry, but I can't feel anything
except the pain of wondering —
Why Danny?

But he would want us to laugh again
And be happy once more.
So let's remember the good times with Danny,
Smile and carry memories of him in our hearts.

I know this in my head and although it is true,
my heart still cries out: Why Danny? Why you?

1985

It was the year I graduated high school, went to college, met my brand-new college roomie when she was in our shower with her boyfriend … fixing the showerhead … met my first real love (we're just friends now) and met my best friend, Suzelle. I wrote a few love poems. These poems I still like.

Lovin' on Borrowed Time

I know you have to go,
so I'll love you while you're here.
There's nothing we can do or say.
It's not going to change.

We're lovin' on borrowed time.
Nothing seems to fit.
There's no reason to this rhyme,
because we're lovin' on borrowed time.

It doesn't matter that we love;
We both have to leave.
We won't keep in touch.
It would hurt too much

I know we can weather
anything when together.
Once apart, our future is unsure.
Let's chuck it all,
run away forever
and chase our dreams by the shore.

But we won't …
because we know
we're lovin' on borrowed time.
Nothing seems to fit.
There's no reason to this rhyme.
We're a hopeless case,
just lovin' on borrowed time.

The Eternal Question

Every day
I ask myself something.
I ask the eternal question:
What is love?

I still don't have an answer.
It isn't something you can see,
hear, touch, taste or smell.
A sense for love is like a sixth sense;
I don't seem to have it.

Am I capable of love?
I wonder.
Do I have the capacity to feel so very deeply?
Or am I cold, like a granite sculpture,
someone not quite human?

I don't think so.
The time is just not right.
Someday I'll know the answer
to the eternal question:
What is love?

1986

The Challenger space shuttle exploded, I met my second love (also still my friend) and I took my first-ever airplane flight at the ripe old age of 19. I white-knuckled it nearly all the way to New York City holding a classmate's hand ... well, that was his story — that he held on in case I was nervous, because I'd told him I never had flown before! I wrote a few more love poems, but none about the classmate who held my hand to NYC.

White Rose

I give you a thornless white rose.
It symbolizes my love for you.
White, because of the pure, perpetual love I feel —
thornless, because ...
I loved you at first sight and never want to hurt you.

The next two poems previously were published in Framework, CMU's now-defunct literary magazine.

Man

He sits,
dreaming —
lost in his own private world.

No one
laughs with him
or shares his sorrow.

Taking refuge
in his usual chair,
he hides behind his newspaper —
trying to conceal
his desolate, barren heart.

When Love Has Gone

When the tumultuous emotion subsides,
when love has gone,
there is left
a vast and curious peace

Where heartache and turmoil once gathered,
there is a space left,
like an empty room,
a room ready for a new love

Pride

There is no place for pride in love,
no space for distant dignity.

Where hurtful pride steps in,
there love never can be.

Pride comes between lovers
who never count the cost

Until love has fled
and hope of its return is lost.

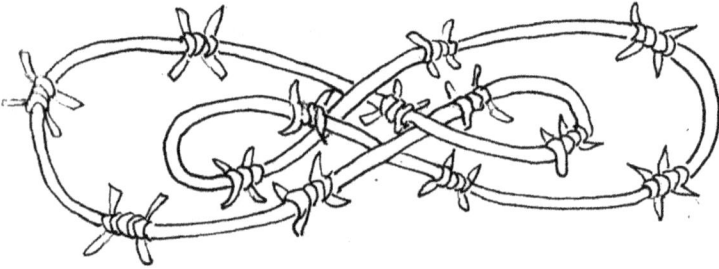

My Fears Realized

Yes, I'm afraid to love
to care about you
to feel down to the marrow of my soul.

How can you tell if love is real
or just a distortion of facts
when our lives
are just a series of acts?

A long time ago, I said no to love.
I ran away from life itself.

Love's mocking echoes followed me
and brought me back.

Love can be a con man's game,
and lovers, pawns in a chess quest for power.
Love has brought more sorrow and shame to the earth
than there are grains in a beach full of sand.

Feeling as if I'm adrift on life's sea —
and that someone just stole my lifejacket —
I want to say no to love once more.
I want to run, fleeing the current of love
that threatens to engulf me, heart and soul.

But it's too late;
all is lost.
Love's tide has won.
But I can't love!
I'm not capable of it ...
am I?

But I do.
Please, God ...

I'm So Afraid

I'm taking a path I've never seen before —
closing the past behind me,
like slamming an open door.
I'm looking to the future.

There's no precedent to follow.
I don't know what to do.
Strangers and strange places
surround me.

Then I see you —
a person I can run to
'cause I'm so afraid —
a link to the past.
I thought it was over.

And I run to you
because I'm so afraid
and lost without you.

But my love for you
scares me even more.
So I run away — again —
Trying to close love's door.

My maternal grandmother, Ruth Magdalen LaBerge (a.k.a. Gram), was a huge influence in my life. After a fall in 1985, she went into a nursing home in November. It was my first year of college. Seeing her in the nursing home was tough on everyone; shortly after her admission there, we learned she had Parkinson's disease. She died three days before my 25th birthday. I also lost my paternal grandfather, Edward Seebaldt, later that year. It wasn't a year I would want to relive.

Grandma's Love

Slow to scold,
quick to praise,
she always has children around
but they're not hers to raise.
Bandaging scrapes
and crying with you over bruises,
handing out peppermints with a smile and kiss —
what kind of love is this?
Grandma's love.
Her own special brand of caring
speaks for itself.
It is uniquely her gift to you.
Treasure it well now,
for it leaves our earth all too soon.

1988

Untitled

I can't begin to describe
what you've come to mean to me
but I can try.

The first day you entered this room
I knew you would be a special friend —
someone who's easy to work and laugh with,
someone trustworthy, sincere and lovable.

It's so comfortable being with you
that we must have known each other before.

I wish you the best as you go out into the world
to find whatever you search for,
but always remember this:
My friendship and caring
Are there whenever you need me.

This was one of the few poems I wrote while I was married. My ex-husband knew I wrote poetry and often wondered why I'd never written one about him. Well, finally I did, but I really don't think it was what he had in mind. We divorced not quite four months later.

April 20, 1997

I'm sitting here with empty arms and an ice cold heart
I wish someone had told me this would happen at the start.
Maybe they did; maybe I just didn't listen.
I feel like I'm left holding the bag again.

I can't respond to your loving arms around me
Hurt has taken over for so long that I almost can't see
Why we even started to see each other
And why we couldn't just keep loving one another.

My heart's not quite broken, but it's badly bruised
You're trying so hard to get through, but is it any use?
I feel almost frozen down to the core
It seems like I can't feel anything but hurt anymore.

I'm not angry; I still care,
but I don't feel like we're going anywhere.
There's an intimate stranger with his arms around me,
but nothing seems to get through to you, so must I go free?

I don't want to leave you here all alone
I worry you won't take care of yourself.
I still care about you, but my heart needs help
It needs intensive care if we're to go on.

I pray to God to let me be
the kind of loving wife you need
But it seems my prayer falls on deaf ears
and all I hear is my heart's answering tears.

2002

I started writing poetry again shortly after I began work at *The Real Estate & Construction Review* in late 1999. Re-reading 2002's *Winter of the Heart*, it is clear I was still wrestling with the pain of divorce.

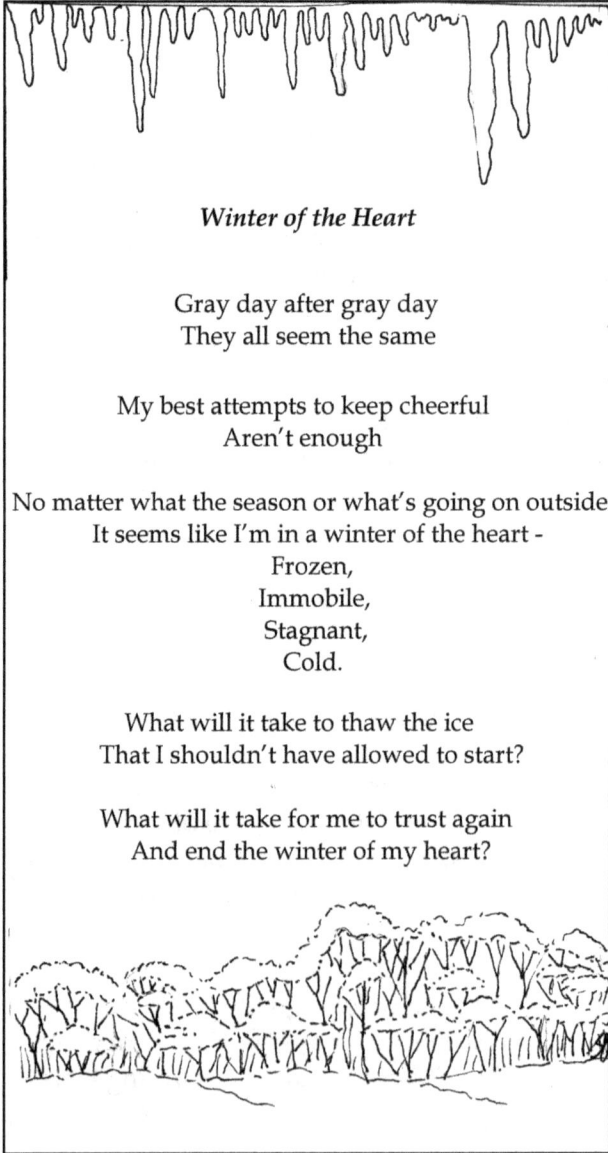

Winter of the Heart

Gray day after gray day
They all seem the same

My best attempts to keep cheerful
Aren't enough

No matter what the season or what's going on outside
It seems like I'm in a winter of the heart -
Frozen,
Immobile,
Stagnant,
Cold.

What will it take to thaw the ice
That I shouldn't have allowed to start?

What will it take for me to trust again
And end the winter of my heart?

2011

You Know

You know my real name,
the one I keep inside me.

You know my true dreams —
the ones I always hide.

You know my deepest thoughts,
and interpret my expression easily,

Uncovering my desires
and helping them to flower.

2013

My Love

My love is vast:
Unending,
Unyielding
And unspoken.

WRITING AND READING

I like to play with words to create poetry. And I have read a lot of poetry. Robert Frost is a favorite and so is Emily Dickinson. (Did you know many of her poems could be sung to the tune of *The Yellow Rose of Texas*? Seriously. Try it sometime.)

All of my poems are reflective of my experiences and observations. I don't do esoteric, highfalutin' poetry. Nor do I use a lot of deliberate symbolism. Whether we love it or hate it, poetry is something that we respond to on a visceral level. It shouldn't be that hard to figure out; it needs to be accessible to people.

1987

Wish I'd Said It

Hoping someday everything will turn around
and I'll come up with an original line.

I hear a song on the radio and wonder
if any lyric I wrote will ever sell.

The greatest lyrics I've ever heard make me feel just fine
I just wish I'd said it first; I wish the thought was mine.

Instead, I used second-hand words, turned to coy phrases;
second-hand thoughts, turned into rhyme.

My perfect thoughts form trite expressions;
Emotionally-charged words turn into paper-bound rhyme.

Still I keep trying to say it;
I'm trying to find the right words
to keep my thoughts in line.
Loving the marriage of pen and paper
Until it comes out wrong again.

And I wish I'd said it right the first time;
Partnered the correct words and feelings
with or without rhyme.

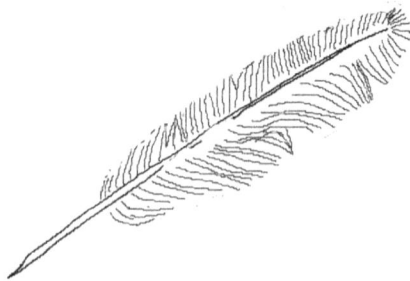

2003

Poet?

What makes a poet a poet and not something else?

A poet finds rhyme — or unrhymed verse —
in everyday things like
a walk in the park
waiting at the doctor's office
standing in line at the bank
working to meet a deadline ...

The poetic form takes those events,
shaping them into phrases
that form a sort of universal experience.

Once, I thought I'd grown too old for it,
that poetry just naturally flows from the young
in angst or alt.

I write poetry by fits and starts,
as the spirit moves me.
I can't seem to write poems
until life sparks incredibly intense feelings within.

Whether it's a happy or sad time
doesn't seem to matter.
Then words flow like a flood
until I've had my say;
and then poetry flees from my soul
to return again another day.

Rhyme has no reason.
Reason has no rhyme,
or so I've been told.

I don't buy that;
a reason is required for me to rhyme

and there is more reason in many rhymes
I've read than in much of what passes for research.

Take your pick — rhymed or unrhymed,
it doesn't really matter
so long as a poem expresses
absolute honesty of the soul.

2009

This poem will boil over if left unattended

Simmering below the surface,
Rhyme romps through my mind, trying desperately to escape.

It meets the brick wall of obligation;
I haven't got the time.

But if I don't seize the moment,
This poem will boil over, left unattended,
leaving nothing but forgotten whispers of what could have been.

Headlines

Large type
Black, white

Announcing fate
Living, dying

Jailed, released
Success, failure

For all
To see.

What I read
In between the lines
Are tales of
Hope,
Despair,
Anger,
Love
And
Hate.

The gamut of emotion
Splayed across the paper
Or computer screen
With the occasional misspelling
In 48-point type (ouch),
Since spell-check can't catch it all.

Mon Petit Escape

A cup of tea next
to me and a book in hand;
it's my ideal escape.

Inhaling the scent
of exotic places tea
grows, I sigh, content.

I'll enjoy a break
in another place and time
from the mundane world.

HAIKU

As a form, haiku has a lot of things going for it. It's short, sweet and to the point. I enjoy the challenge of the economy of words essential to it with its sparse 5-7-5 syllable pattern. I can state definitively that writing haikus is something even elementary students can enjoy, because I have taught this art to fourth and fifth graders.

1982

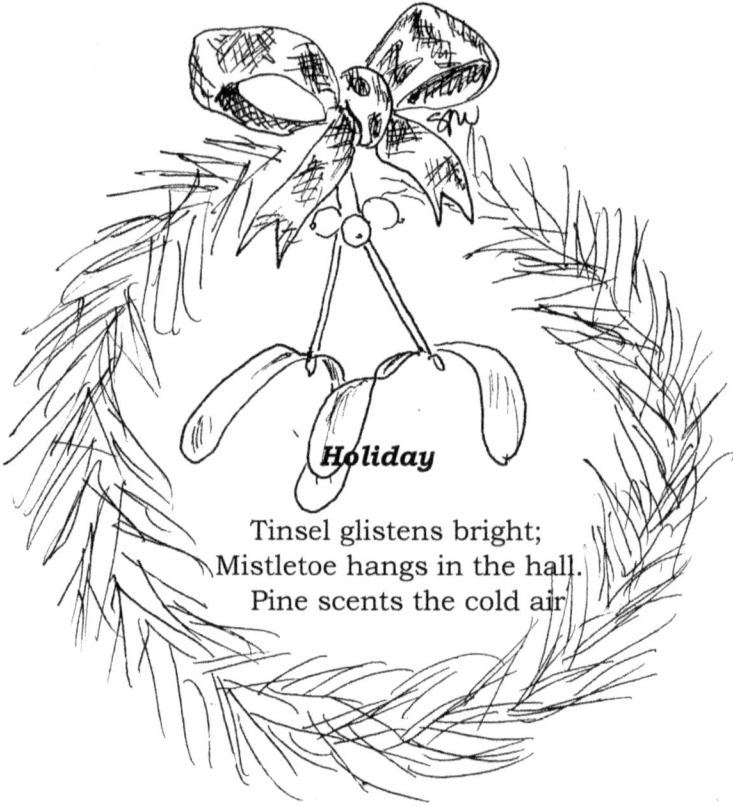

Holiday

Tinsel glistens bright;
Mistletoe hangs in the hall.
Pine scents the cold air

2009

Beware of poem: a double haiku
Beware of poem
Creeping up on you at night
Keeping you awake.

Write it all down now;
Let fancy escape your mind;
Allow dreams to soar.

This is Not a Poem

"Not poetry – life"
He explained disdainfully.
"Same thing," I told him.

Do you Haiku?

Some will say haiku
Is much too brief, and lacks rhyme;
they don't understand

It is the essence,
Heart laid bare for all to see
Exposing what's true.

Natural as breath,
Eating, drinking or sleeping:
Friend, do you haiku?

2014

Writing Groove

My pencil flies past
the first line, and the second
in the writing groove.

PHILOSOPHY, FAITH AND THE NATURAL WORLD

I have always addressed my own personal philosophy, faith and
nature in my poetry and have always been greatly affected by
natural beauty, especially that of water. I am such a water baby; it is
almost ridiculous. I have swum in Lake Huron's Tawas Bay in early
June; that is how crazy I am about water! The very first poem I
wrote about nature, *The Forest Door*, was so real to me that I felt I
was walking through that forest when I wrote it.

1983

The Forest Door

Reeds sway, bent by the river.
The brilliant sun is a life giver.
Berries shine — little jeweled clusters on a vine.
The river runs, clear as glass, free of all grime.

Glossy green leaves grow from the forest floor.
Sunlight shines in like a glowing door.
Fair flowers grace banks of clay.
And a gentle breeze helps a traveler on his way.

1984

Gifted

They say that I'm "gifted."
That could be.
But all my life I've heard
I don't work to my ability.

Other kids call me a "brain."
They treat me differently
Than the "normal" kids.
They won't let me be me.

Why can't they see
That I'm just another kid?
Trying to grow up like other people did.

Everyone's different.
Everybody is unique.
So what if he's short and she's tall;
If you're big and I'm small?

Please don't judge others by color, creed or I.Q.
Then I can be me and you can be you.

1986

Family

We are brother, sister, father, mother, aunt, uncle,
niece, nephew, cousins, and Grandpa;
Sometimes we argue about unimportant trivia.

But through it all
a lasting love abides;
we're there when another member calls.
Despite everything, we can't hide
that we're a family.

Someone Comes Along

Every time life seems it can't go on,
Someone comes along to make it worthwhile.

Just keep your eyes open or you may miss that chance.

Whenever dreams are shattered,
Someone will pick up the pieces and make you smile.

Keep an open mind, because a better dream
might be around the corner.

If confidence is destroyed, someone comes along
To help you rebuild it.

Keep trusting, even when it seems
you can't do anything right. You will.

For every broken heart,
There is someone to mend it.

So keep your heart open; don't close yourself off from everyone.

For every hurt,
There is someone to end it.

Keep going so you meet the right person at the right time to help you.

Every time you lose your way,
Someone comes along to help you find it again.

A friend's input might be just the road map you need.

Someone is always around
To help you ease life's pain.

God's love is expressed by people every day.
Just wait and watch for it.

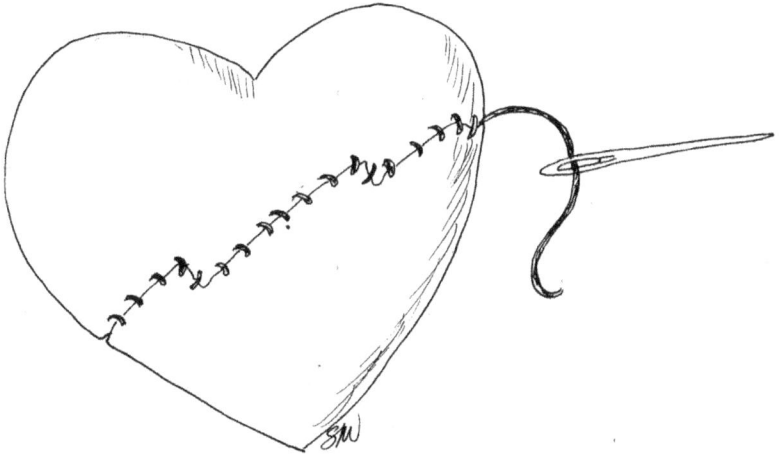

1988

Souls

Our souls touched
the first time I saw you.

Knowing you makes me a better person.
Your gentle influence acts on me
without need of words.
Your forthright yet kind personality
makes shy people bloom like spring flowers.

You make me more acutely aware
of the world and its surrounding beauty —
now I notice the flowers,
twice as vivid and lovely as ever before —
even in the midst of busy traffic and a frantic crowd.

Despite the short time since we met,
you are a dear friend.
It was meant for us to meet.

I'm so glad you touched my life and my heart.
You make a world of difference.

Call it Kismet, call it whatever you like — but our souls touched,
finding an instant rapport and an eternal bond of friendship.

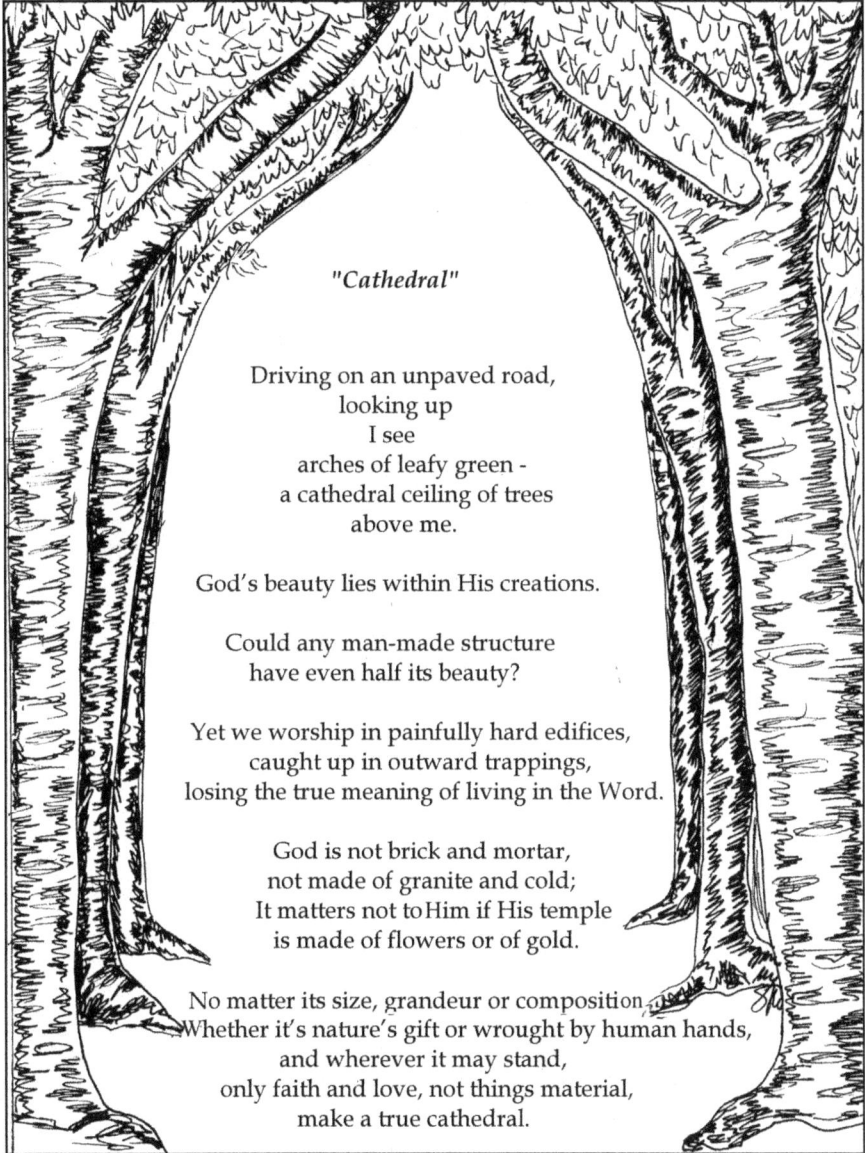

"Cathedral"

Driving on an unpaved road,
looking up
I see
arches of leafy green -
a cathedral ceiling of trees
above me.

God's beauty lies within His creations.

Could any man-made structure
have even half its beauty?

Yet we worship in painfully hard edifices,
caught up in outward trappings,
losing the true meaning of living in the Word.

God is not brick and mortar,
not made of granite and cold;
It matters not to Him if His temple
is made of flowers or of gold.

No matter its size, grandeur or composition
Whether it's nature's gift or wrought by human hands,
and wherever it may stand,
only faith and love, not things material,
make a true cathedral.

Trophy

When I wander through the night
I wonder if there is a man
who looks on a woman
without considering her
as a potential prize.

Is there a man
who doesn't want to be my master
who isn't out to find
a trophy to show off to his friends
then discard her like a child's toy?

In a world where violence is common,
are there any gentle men,
men who want a friend and lover,
not some kind of slave?
I wonder who and where they are,
if they exist, maybe
on some far-off star?

I am more than some man's trophy.
I have my own identity.
I deserve respect;
I deserve to be treated with care and dignity.
I am not anyone's toy.

Do not try to belittle me
because you think it makes you a man.
Real men don't need to hurt others.
They treat people with respect,
and their behavior commands respect from others.

Too Much Faith?

In this world
I see little reason,
much less rhyme,
and no real faith
in the goodness of mankind.

Still I have faith
that humans
are basically sound;
we all have hearts,
ambitions, dreams
that lie buried inside us
like a treasure
in the cold, hard ground.

Maybe I have too much faith
in the benevolence of man,
thinking idealistically
that, when it's time,
we will reach out
to give each other a hand.

Maybe that's too much to ask,
but there's nothing worth
keeping alive for eternity
except faith, love, and hope.

1990

Hate
Hate is an emotion
unworthy of the name.

Seeds of hate,
when planted and nurtured,
grow into a flourishing
tree of death, destruction and evil.

The fires of hate
burn down the soul
to nothing but
dust and ash.

2001

Forgiveness
Forgiveness is a funny thing.
Most of us find it easy to take
and much harder to give.

But who is hurt more —
those who don't forgive
or those who are not forgiven?

Forgiveness is a cleansing thing.
It fills you with a sense of rebirth,
allowing you to move forward.

When did I forgive
those I thought I never could,
when I'd tried and failed so many times?

I really don't know.
It crept into my heart slowly
making me whole once more.

Only in Your Mind

Helter skelter …
My brain just won't turn off.

The wheels won't stop grinding
no matter how I tell it to stop.

Going here, going there,
calling him, writing that.
Concentration is the key.
Now what was the question?

Does reality intrude upon you,
crashing from outside in?
Or is reality simply that
which is only in your mind?

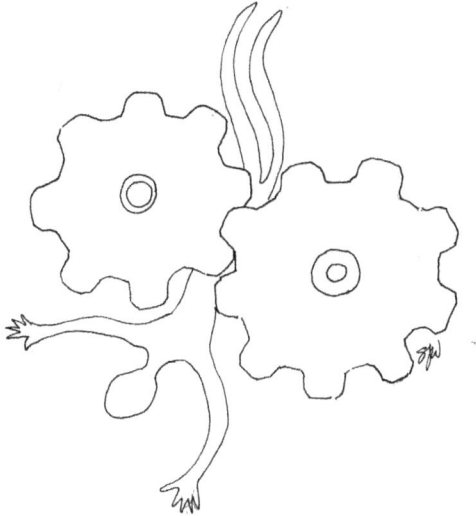

Wishes

May I be as hardy and resilient
as a dandelion.

No matter how many times
it is cut down,
it springs up again.

May I be able to
wind my way around difficulties
as easily as a violet transcends
the boundaries with which
we try to confine it to one space,
wandering into and beautifying the grass.

2003

Just a Thought

While into my life
some rain must fall,
it's good to know
my friends have umbrellas
to stop the rain
from drenching us all.

2010

Trust

The building block
of all relationships,
trust is easily broken
and much harder to repair.

We need to be honest
With ourselves and others.

God? Fate? Karma?

Karma,
Fate, God, Kismet —
whatever we call it, we know it
when we see it
come in — or out —
of our lives and our hearts.

What's meant to be, is,
whether you want it or not.
Some say it's Fate
I give credit to God.

2012

TV

Kids complain,
"There's nothing to watch!"

I laugh silently,
thinking of a time
when if the President
gave a speech,
I missed a program
I'd looked forward to
all week long.

It's all there,
in digital Technicolor:
more than 200 channels of
drama,
passion,
hate,
love,
in your living room,
night after endless night;
you would be better served by
doing nearly anything else.

2013

Genetically-modified? I'll pass.

I do not like these G.M. seeds
not even if they resist weeds
I do not like them in the ground
I do not like them all around.
I do not want to eat their fruit
I do not like them; that's the truth.

WHAT DOES FREEDOM MEAN?

What Does Freedom Mean? was written as part of *Connected,* a larger exhibit that was featured at the 2013 Grand Rapids ArtPrize event. Each artist-writer team selected a random word that was to inspire their work. This is by far the longest poem I have written.

What Does Freedom Mean?

Canto I

Just as a Bald Eagle lifts off a tree branch
And soars the skies in freedom
A boy rides his bike to the Fourth of July parade,
Red, white and blue ribbons on his basket
And his uncle's Purple Heart pinned to his shirt.

He hears The Star-Spangled Banner
Play as veterans walk through the street,
Receiving the applause they didn't get
When they returned from 'Nam.

His mother had told him once
How the first parade she saw
Included Vietnam veterans,
Among them his uncle,
The one who earned a Purple Heart.

They were pelted with rotten
Fruits and vegetables
For a war they fought in
And had little choice but to enter.
Where was their freedom?

We know freedom isn't free.
But it's easy to be distracted
By the lure of the long weekend,
By good food, family and friends,
Forgetting the very people
We should celebrate.

Kids skid around with sparklers,
Play tag, or swim.
Picnics abound,
And as the sun goes down,

You hear loud sounds
Of fireworks lighting the sky.

There aren't too many who
Make the time to show
Their appreciation of those
Who fought our wars,
And did the hard thing —
Many of whom never came home —
Some for a cause they didn't believe in.
But they did their duty
So we could enjoy freedom's benefits.

Canto II

What symbolizes freedom to you:

Cornwallis surrendering,
A Revolution won
Our country freed
From the tyranny
Of a far-away power?

Or Lincoln freeing the slaves?

How about Rosa Parks keeping her seat on the bus,
Or the March on Washington with Dr. King?

Think of our rights as outlined
By the Constitution and the Bill of Rights.
Is it freedom of speech, assembly and press
That which makes America uniquely free?

Maybe you think the Star-Spangled Banner
Sung before the baseball game
Is the best symbol of our freedom?

Do your thoughts turn to the amazing sight
Of that Bald Eagle flying high over the horizon,
Rare, beautiful, and awe-inspiring?

Could having the ability
To think the way you want,
Worship as you wish (or not),
Freedom from the will of the minority,
Be what truly frees us?

Canto III

How does freedom feel?
Is it something deep inside,
An elemental, basic, raw emotion?

Or perhaps it's an abstract concept
Hard for many to truly grasp?

Is your freedom *from* something,
like personal tyranny?

An escape from the bondage of drugs?

Freedom from thinking you're powerless,
Giving you the ability to *do* something,
Such as attend college,
Make a better living than your parents
While pursuing the American Dream?

Is the price we have paid for our freedom too high?
How about the price we paid for others' freedom,
For those who might not even want our help?
Those who will simply go back to war with one another,
As they have been for hundreds, maybe even thousands of years,
After our troops finally come back to their families?

Perhaps we value freedom too cheaply —
The soldiers lost, the money squandered.
Are we fighting a just war?
Are our losses acceptable?
And if they are, who finds them so?

Are we giving up too many of our rights
For "homeland security?"

Maybe there really isn't
Any such thing as freedom
Except the freedom
To choose our own prison bars,
While having the choice to think and feel
Without relying upon others' opinions.

As Gloria Steinem once said,
"The truth will set you free, but first it will piss you off."

www.ingramcontent.com/pod-product-compliance
Lightning Source LLC
Chambersburg PA
CBHW060617030426

42337CB00018B/3086